Poems & Devotionals to Help Soothe All that is Chaotic

Renewal of Joy

Alma L. Carr-Jones

© 2021 Alma L. Carr-Jones

Paperback ISBN-13: 978-1-948026-82-6
Digital ISBN-13: 978-1-948026-83-3

All rights reserved. No part of this publication may be reproduced or transmitted in any form or by any means without written permission from the publisher.

Unless otherwise noted, Scriptures are taken from the Holy Bible, New International Version®, NIV®. Copyright © 1973, 1978, 1984, 2011 by Biblica, Inc.™ Used by permission of Zondervan. All rights reserved worldwide. www.zondervan.com.

Scripture quotations marked "KJV" are from the King James Version by public domain.

Scripture quotations marked "NKJV" are taken from The New King James Version / Thomas Nelson Publishers, Nashville: Thomas Nelson Publishers., Copyright © 1982. Used by permission. All rights reserved.

Published by TMP Books, 3 Central Plaza Ste 307, Rome, GA 30161
www.TMPBooks.com

Dedicated to

All who have lost loved ones to Covid-19.
All who have lost health to Covid-19.
All who have been shut in for over a year.
All who have kept the faith and kept smiles in spite of.
All who kept stepping on with the church of tomorrow in mind.

And most of all to The Almighty GOD of lovingkindness, justice, and righteousness, WHO welcomes us to HIS Throne by many Bible passages, to include Hebrews 4:16.

Acknowledgements

I want to extend grateful thanks to all who have supported, pushed, and encouraged me on my writing journey.

Table of Contents

A Note from the Author 3
Devotional: Father, I Thank You 5
Devotional: Together We Raise 7
Devotional: Storms (from Chopping My Row) 9
Devotional: You Can Do It 25
Poem: It's a Wrap 31
Devotional: Momma and the Rent Man 33
Devotional: Just Dust 43
Devotional: Sweating Tears 45
Devotional: Come Boldly unto the Throne of Grace 49
Devotional: Begin Your Day with Prayer 51
Devotional: Guiding Hand 53
Devotional: Faith Moves Mountains 55
Devotional: The Glory of GOD 57
Devotional: Another Stop on the Road to Ultimately 59
Devotional: Improving Today for All My Tomorrows 61
Devotional Poem: Your Name I Do Praise 65
Poem: His Will 66
Poem: My Father 67
Devotional: Uncomfortable 69
Shape Poem: Your Road 71
Poem: 7 Days 73
Poem: The Word, "Momma" 75
Poem: Renewed Faith in My Fellowman 79
Devotional: Influence 85
About the Author 89
Other Books by the Author 90

A Note from the Author:

Hello precious neighbor. I have penned some devotionals and poems for your quick perusal and pick-me-up during these arduous times. It is my aim that these poems and devotionals reach into your psyche and soothe all that is chaotic, and bring a renewal of joy where joy used to reside. It is my hope that these pieces act as the care package (a package orchestrated by the machinations of the Lord's Holy Spirit) that you may have been long hoping for and expecting from the Lord. May your soul be blessed, your spirit renewed, and your joy heightened as you partake of this offering given to you for the glory of GOD.

~ *Alma*

Alma L. Carr-Jones

Devotional:
Father, I Thank You

Father I thank You
For the love that carries me day by day
    (love that has kept me going)
And for the blood of Jesus that cleanses me along my way
    (keeps me in touch with You no matter my sin)
For a lifetime of awe, wonder, blessings and care
    (my whole life, Lord my whole life!)
Thank You, Dear GOD for always being there.
    (faithful Father)
And when I get to that city where you dwell
    (when I make it in)
If I am allowed to, I will look at Your Presence
    (If I can just glimpse Your glory…)
And give back the love, care packages, keepings
    (Thank You)
Sacrifices and all that you have lavished on me
I will send You a lifetime of thanksgiving
    (All to You)
For all the treasure that You heaped upon
Me while I was, as a piece of dust, living.

I would send that love to the proper channels
    (seraphim)
So that it could be cleaned up and added as
Another ornament of praise and adoration
    (an ornament of my heartfelt praise would be added for Alma)
To float in Your Presence in the Heavenly majestic air
Along with the countless others that are already there
Amen.

Alma L. Carr-Jones

There are times in life that I am touched so deeply that words roll through my spirit and congeal into crystal thought. The poem above is an example of one such time. When I think about the love and care that has been shown to me throughout my lifetime, I get filled with the need to say, "I love You back." But then I realize how inadequate my words would be because they cannot give true love to the GOD of All Creation. So, I penned the poem above to show my Father and you the love that I have for Him. I wanted to tell Him that He deserves to be praised always. I wanted to tell Him, "Thank You," for allowing me, this piece of dust, to serve Him and to praise Him. I wanted to tell Him that though I don't always do as I should, I thank Him for His forgiveness, love, and for His continual grace in my life.

Each day that I live, I want to realize that my purpose is to bring glory to my Father and to proclaim His love to all. I have to realize that this is paramount to the message of love that I must bring to humanity. I had to realize a long time ago, that life is not all about "I, me, or my." I had to learn to put myself on the back burner, so to speak, and live to proclaim the goodness of and live for the Omnipotent One. To GOD Be the Glory. Amen.

Devotional:
Together We Raise

I do things that may be a bit unorthodox from time to time. But, that's okay because my intent is heartfelt and genuine. "Uh oh," is what you are probably thinking; "What is she up to now?" I thought that I would let you participate as I begin my day with prayer, thereby Beginning YDWP. If you are reading this and it is not the beginning of your day, not to worry, we have covered that contingency, as well. Here we go...

Good morning, Jesus. It's me, Alma. I humbly come before your throne in thankfulness and in supplication, but I did not come alone. I bring several of my readers from countries around the world with me. And while they might not address you as Jesus as I do, according to their various languages, we come as individuals, and we come with a united purpose. We come to say, "Thank You" and we come in supplication.

We thank you for every nuance of the plan that you made for our lives and for Your bringing us to this moment in that plan. We thank you for every direction that the wind did blow us in (even the Covid-19 winds) as we realize that the various gales that we have encountered have brought us closer to you and to this moment of individual and collective thanks. We thank you that every wind that we encountered was not a gale, but sometimes gentle breezes of, "Rest now, child; I still have My hands on you." For Your lovingkindness, we say, "Thank You, Lord!"

Lord, I have come a long way from that starry eyed little girl that you allowed to flourish in a Memphis ghetto. And though life has tossed me to and fro, You have kept, coddled, nurtured and yes, even chastised me into being the woman that I am today. I open my heart in the presence of my readers to acknowledge, praise and thank You. This is one of the ways that I am and will shout out my love, adoration and thankfulness to You, before all mankind. And, am I ashamed? Nope, not in the least! It is proud I am to say, "He is my GOD and Lord of all!" My readers join me in this sentiment.

In the supplication portion of my prayer, I ask that You accept this prayer of mine, even if the form may not be as exact as it should be. Please bless each individual (no matter the time) reading this with a purpose united with us, with the blessing(s) that we each stand in need of as you bless the sale of and acceptance of this book. May this book bring praise to You and bless people of all cultures to continue to embrace You and those that don't embrace You, to get to know and to love You. May this book help to unite us all under the roof of Your love, as we are all Your creation. May the love for You that I have tried to encapsulate in this book, touch hearts and nurture the spirits of mankind the world over. And thank You, Lord, that you allowed some of the stars in my eyes to remain and the lost stars to be replaced by shimmering beams of hope. It is in Jesus' name that I pray, Amen.

For Pondering:

Why is this piece entitled, "Together We Raise"?

Devotional:

Storms

(from *Chopping My Row*)

LESSON 2: Storms (Isaiah 41:13 NKJV)

Aim: To realize that though trouble and trials are a part of the Christian life, we are never alone. To learn how to handle times of adversity.

Song: "Shelter in the Time of a Storm"

Sometimes we have to go through some rough things in life, either things we bring on ourselves or things that people cause to happen to us. At times we can be so beaten down that it is hard to keep the upbeat feeling that we started off with, huh? Well, we are going to be dealing with storms in this lesson, but I want to begin by saying a couple of things to you:

1. You must never think that giving your heart and soul to the Lord means that the adversary is going to stop bothering you. Nothing could be further from the truth. Remember Job.

2. The second thing to remember is to give all your problems to Him, and don't pick them back up again. This is covered in more detail in lesson 8, Chopping My Row.

Now, let's work through storms and how to handle them, shall we? As soon as something we don't like or don't understand happens in our lives, most of us question the Lord: "Is He listening? Can He hear me? Does He care?" Y'all know how we do sometimes. But what we need to remember is that sometimes the adversary uses storms to weaken our faith. Haven't you ever noticed how many times the adversary kicks us when we are down? He does that because he knows that if we believe the Lord no longer hears us, we will cease to pray, thereby damaging our relationship with GOD. So, he will go after us just like he did Job. You see, when you are committed to GOD as Job was, the adversary knows it.

The adversary figures that if he can get the "Job" in the church, he can get the rest of us. It seems as if every time you get your head above water, something else happens, and you are right back where you started. Never forget that GOD is omnipotent; nothing happens without His permission (Job 1:12; Lamentations 3:37–38 NKJV), and nothing surprises or confuses Him, not even a pandemic. When we have setbacks, we must remember that they are temporary. After all, "All things work together for good for those that love the Lord" (Romans 8:28 KJV NKJV).

In lesson 1 we learned that the Lord has a plan for our lives. Well, use that piece of information to keep you strong. This GOD you are questioning now is the same GOD that brought you through your yesterdays. This same GOD is the One of whom the disciples asked, "What manner of man is this that even the wind and sea obey Him?" This same GOD is the One Who took the plagues away from Egypt.

Mark Your Storm in Green

I recommend highlighting the above underlined phrase in green to remind you that as long as grass grows green from season to season, GOD is in control and there is a reason for the turmoil in your life, because He plans things out to benefit you and some other woman or man, simultaneously.

Just like a teacher crafts a lesson for her students with a primary objective in mind, she always remembers other concepts that have not been mastered by the kids yet and builds, within the lesson, supplementary exercises to strengthen any remaining weaknesses that the lesson might find.

That being said, you know that the Lord is the Master Teacher, for sure, so realize that anything that He has you go through is according to His masterful plan to bless and affect some needed cure.

The Adversary Has Chosen You

What do you do when you figure out that the adversary has chosen you for an onslaught? You have to stick close to the Lord at all times. This means that when troubles come at you all at once and you have to contend with decades worth of trouble all piling up at once, you talk to

GOD more than ever! This may be one of those times when even your friends get tired of trying to lift you up, just as Job's friends got tired. But you must keep going! If you have the presence of mind to realize that what is happening to you is just not normal, then have the presence of mind to know that there is a Supreme Supernatural Force that no one and nothing can get the best of. Just remember that He sees, He cares, He is on the job, and He never rests from protecting His children.

Standing on Top of the Mountain

Standing on top of the mountain feeling blessed,
Standing on the top of the mountain feeling no stress,
Fell from the mountaintop to the valley
And couldn't see the light of day.
But, you know what?
Carried Jesus with me every step of the way!

Strength Gone

I'm glad that His love covers me in all my weakness and my trials, for when my strength is tried and gone, His strengthening power takes hold and carries me on.

Weed Problems on the Row

Back in lesson 1, we talked about some of the weeds you can run into when chopping a row of cotton, namely cockleburs, morning glories, and Johnson grass. I chose the metaphor of cotton chopping because I did a little of it as a child, and I remember how tiresome and tedious it could be. Even when I finally learned how to chop cotton properly, I still was not very good at it, because in order to be good at it, you had to have a keen eye for spotting the morning glory vines that grew in with the cotton. If you did not cut off the vines at ground level, they would grow all tangled and entwined in the cotton, stunting its growth. I learned that cutting them off at the ground stopped their spread, and they would die and choke the cotton no longer.

Then there was the problem of cockleburs. I learned to chop them down when they were young and toss them in the row middle, where they caused no more trouble. I learned quickly not to get entangled in the cockleburs, because they stuck any place they could and were quite painful to get out of clothing and hair.

Oh, but what about that Johnson grass? That stuff was a hot mess to deal, with, as my friend Mitzi would say. We were always told to dig Johnson grass up by the root. Let's take this grass and break down the trouble it caused in a row, shall we? The Johnson grass would stunt the growth of the cotton plant, so it had to be removed. When I use Johnson grass in the metaphor of Christians trying to work on a row in the Lord's vineyard, doing what they have been given to do in this Christian life, I liken it to when a supercell storm hits our life. Above, when I mentioned being faced with decades worth of trouble in a matter of months, that is analogous to encountering Johnson grass. This definition of the grass illustrates why farmers detest it so much: "Perennial with vigorous rhizomes. Coarse, rapidly growing, difficult to control grass that reaches up to 2 m tall. Plants can rapidly develop colonies. Johnson grass, considered one of the 10 most noxious weeds in the world, is especially troublesome in cotton fields. Infestations of the grass in crops, because it is competitive with them, can reduce harvest yields significantly" (Texas Invasives).

I remember a few lessons about dealing with Johnson grass in my youth that can apply to _____:

1. The first step is to make sure your hoe is sharpened to the max. (Make sure that you are prayed up.)

2. Make sure you eat a good lunch. (Make sure that you are read up in your Bible.)

3. Get some extra help with chopping the grass. (Find prayer partners to help you make it through the storms, because the Bible says, "The prayers of the righteous availeth much" [James 5:16 KJV).

4. Be prepared for your muscles to be sore when you get through the patch. (Be prepared for the "Doesn't GOD love us?" blues to settle in.)

5. Rub in some liniment as necessary. (Worship services will soothe the battered muscles of your faith. Preachers had to be extra thoughtful and prayerful in handling this with the pandemic.)

If you are battling a particularly nasty storm right now, allow me to say that I know you feel like it's going to kill you; I did too. I know you feel like you can't take it; I did too. I know you feel like this will make you crazy; I thought so too. Often, I had to cry the way I saw my mother do when I was a little girl. There have been times during prayer when I have had tears sliding down my face as I talked to my Father.

But through it all, though I wrung my hands, though I cried and prayed, I kept my faith. As a matter of fact, usually by the end of my prayer, my faith had kicked up to its highest level (ramrod strong). I began to wait on the Lord. I read my Bible daily, and I waited and prayed on a continuous basis (Psalm 27:14 and Isaiah 40:31). So, too, you must endure. Your breakthrough/anointing is on the other side of the trouble you are walking or crawling through. Your only way out is to go through it.

Remember the poem above that gave you stepping-on power when it told you to paint your storms green. And then, sister, you step on anyway!

Nowhere to Run

Sometimes in our battle to be a good soldier for the Lord, we come to the intersection of two streets called Nowhere to Run and Nowhere to Hide. Remember the fact that David had to run and then had to hide in a cave to keep Saul from killing him (1 Samuel 22:1 NKJV). Then you think about Jesus and remember that He said that "He is going to wipe all our tears away" (Revelation 21:4) when we get Home. That's one thing that we have to remember; despite all the world's current problems, trials, and heartaches, all we have to do is make it Home. Then we think about the times the Lord has brought us through before. It will help us to remember the words of that old song that says, "All that I am and ever hope to be, I owe it all to Thee."

That means that all I am, claim to be, and am *gonna* be is because of the Lord. The two preceding sentences should refer our minds back to the plan that the Lord has for our lives (Lesson 1, Jeremiah 29:11 KJV; Psalm 37:23; Proverbs 16:9; 1 Corinthians 2:9 NKJV).

Alma L. Carr-Jones

'People Are Watching Me' Battle Scars

Have gained some battle scars in my skirmishes with the adversary, but would do it all again if told, though of the enemy I'm wary (excerpt from Excelsior.)

Think You Can't Make It

So, you think you cannot make it. I tell you that is just not so. Listen to me, sister of mine, And I'll tell you what I know.

Let me tell you a little story about something that happened in my life.

On April 16, 1987, my house burned down. The fire was so hot that it even burned up the floor. If you have never experienced a house fire, you have no true idea of the trauma it wreaks on your life. It will attack you in ways you never even thought about. It will shake your faith to the core. You will find that you miss things you had previously taken for granted, such as your children's baby pictures.

You will think about them and cry. But then you will remember the Scripture Job 14:14 NKJV.

Remember when I told you to always look for your blessing in your storm?

Job 14:14 NKJV is a good reference Scripture for that. Read it. Start thinking about what possible good can come out of the chaos or trouble in which you find yourself.

Below are some blessings that came from my house fire, some of which I realized then; other realizations came years later.

- There was no loss of life in the fire. At the time of the fire, my babies were at school, my husband was at work, and I was in my classroom teaching.

- My mother, bless her heart, was in her own house next door at the time of the fire, which engulfed both homes. The tip end of one of her plaits burned off—and that is all. When I got home that day, she was standing across the road from the blazing house, along with some of the other neighbors, looking dazed, as if she could not believe this had happened. The fire had already burned her house to the ground and was well on its way to devouring mine. But she was okay! I got to have my Momma for seventeen more blessed years. When she did die, I realized what the Lord had not allowed the fire to take from me that April day. (Her leaving me is a narrative for another time, but suffice it to say that I did not know anything could hurt that badly.)

- Our cat's paws got scorched, and it had to spend a couple of days at the vet, but it was okay too. It lived to a ripe old life after the fire.

- I vowed that if I ever got any more china, I would use it regularly and not leave it sitting up in the china cabinet waiting for some special occasion.

- I cried a lot over the lost pictures of my kids, but various family members and friends brought me copies that I had given to them.

- We had no insurance at the time, but these days we are insurance poor!

- We have had several riding mowers since the loss of the brand new one that we had spent all our income tax return on.

- The kids' schools supplied them with new bikes and clothes.

- My school took care of my clothes and the kitchenware and replaced a precious broom I cried so much over. As a matter of fact, I received three brooms!

- Church members, black and white (there's a lesson in that for us today), supplied everything else—and I do mean everything else. It was common for someone to walk up to me and ask what else I needed or to shake my hand and leave it graced with a $100 bill. I still have a mental picture of three church members bringing a brand new couch and armchair into my house. I never knew people could care that much. That outpouring of love across racial barriers put a smile on my face. I think it was GOD's way of sending me a care package— one of those tailor-made blessings with your name written all over it (more about this in lesson 8). I have never forgotten the feeling of receiving the gift. I also have never forgotten that people will watch you to see how you handle your adversity— and your reaction to your own storm might just be a blessing for somebody with a storm headed their way.

- We stayed with my husband, Paul's aunt and uncle for two nights after the fire and then moved to a little yellow house on a hill in the heart of Martin. It even had a washing machine— not as nice as the one I had, but a washing machine, nevertheless.

- My mother was given her own apartment, for which she was very thankful.

- This experience taught me that people will look at you to see how you handle a situation in your times of stress. I repeated this item because I want you to be very aware of it. Our reactions do speak for or against the Lord, even in these historic times.

Must Remember

Must remember that people are watching me
As I travel along life's highway.
Must remember that I might influence someone
By what I do and what I say.

Earlier, I told you about a lady who complimented me because my faith stayed strong during the time of my fire— you know, losing so much, and no insurance to boot. She thought it was outstanding that I could have a smile on my face during that time. She told me she wished she had a faith that strong. I thanked her and kept moving. Well, about seven to eight months later, this same lady was diagnosed with stage-four cancer. She lived less than a year after her diagnosis.

She told me something I will remember as long as the Lord allows my thought processes to flow: "Alma, come here a minute, I want to talk to you," she said to me one day. "I just wanted to tell you, Alma, that I admire you. Yes, I know that shocks you, but I do. This is why I admire you. Back in the spring, when your house burned, you kept a smile on your face. And now I can have that same strong faith that you displayed. That is how I am making it through this cancer and the ravages it has put my life and my body through. So Alma, I just wanted to say thank you."

Folks, I have never forgotten the lesson she taught me that day, even though she did not realize she was teaching me one. And that is why you will often hear me say, "Be a blessing to others in their storm, even though you are going through storms of your own—because, ladies, we just don't know why we are going through what we go through."

Several years after my house fire, one of the teachers at my new school (new because I had moved to a different job in a regular classroom in a different school after so many years of praying) lost her home to a fire. Since the school where I was moved was the one that had bought new clothes and a bike for my son, they knew that I had suffered a fire several years back. Therefore, they came to me with a request that I list some things the teacher would need after a fire. I listed what I thought was needed, and I reiterated, again and again, the need to take her a broom. Most everyone scoffed at the idea and would not do it. They took all kinds of things, big and little. When they got to her she was overwhelmed with gratitude, but she burst out crying, saying, guess what? You got it: "But I don't even have a broom!" They sent some of the men pronto to get that broom, along with a mop and dustpan, etc. They all said, "Alma told us to get a broom!" Now, here is the point I wanted to make with the broom scenario. If I had never experienced a house fire, I would not have known the absolute lostness, the sense of floundering you feel and the necessity of bringing a broom to the victim of the fire. That fire taught me how to be empathetic in a way I would not have been had I not suffered a house fire of my own.

This experience taught me that "All things work together for good for those that love the Lord" (Romans 8:28 NKJV). Though the fire was not a comfortable or enjoyable experience for me, it taught me to lean on the Lord in a way that I never had. I had always been close to the Lord and knew it, or so I thought, but this fire taught me a level of dependence on faith that I had never known. And it taught me a vulnerability I had not had since becoming an adult.

Be a blessing to someone else in their storm, even though you are going through storms of your own.

Ultimately

Ultimately. What a word! What a word! What does this word mean, and why am I so fascinated by it? Just hold your horses, and I will tell you why I love this word so much. I hope that when I finish my explanation you will feel the same way about it. The word ultimate is defined as maximum, final, or supreme. I like to say that it refers to a time "when all has been said and all has been done—the buck stops here." Now, I want you to hold onto that thought for me, because I am going someplace with it. I'll be there in a minute or so. All I ask you to do for me is this: if, at the end of this lesson, your load has been lightened or if you have been given a better perspective on handling stressful situations, then pass the blessing on to somebody else. That's all I ask, okay? All right, here we go!

I was not there when "the foundation of the earth was laid, its measurements were set, its bases were sunk, and its cornerstone laid. I was not there when the morning stars sang together, and all the sons of GOD shouted for joy" (Job 38). I am not going to take the time to cite the entire chapter here, but you would do well to revisit it if you haven't read it lately. Whenever I am going through trying times in my life, I read that passage, and then I talk to my FATHER, and this is the gist of what I say to HIM:

Owing to your faithfulness, FATHER, I know that everything in my life is going to be okay, because you have already told me so in your word. I have just finished reading from the book of Job 38 NKJV, so I repent, FATHER, for the times, as now, when I think, 'This isn't fair, what's happening to me. But I didn't do anything.' I am so sorry and ask YOU to forgive me. You see, FATHER, I forgot to remember that though it is hard right now, it is still not the charcoal-bucket days - (days in the dead of winter that our lights, gas and water had been disconnected because my mother did not have the money to pay it)— that, ultimately, You have control of everything that happens in my life. I also know that when Job was going through his trials, nothing could happen to him without Your say-so. YOU limited how much the adversary could do to him, just as you limit how much turmoil the adversary can inflict upon me. I also know that YOU brought Job through okay. But you didn't stop there. Just as a mother prepares for a new baby, in all Your wisdom You created hope for me when You had Job's story recorded. You have shown Your love in everything You have done for us, especially through Your Son, Jesus.

You not only had the Bible written for us, but you made sure Scripture told us that the Bible contains "Everything that pertains to life and godliness." And then you had it further say that "Whatsoever things that were written before time were written for our learning." (Romans 15:4 KJV) It is no coincidence the Bible contains examples and stories for us that we turn to often for encouragement and spiritual nourishment. After all, You had the Bible prepared for us with love. I am proud to be living during the time of free Bible reading, and in a country where there is no penalty of death for exercising our right to serve You.

A prayer for the journey so far: Thank You, Father, and forgive me when I complain about the storms in my life. I will keep reminding myself of all the preparations that you have made for me, and I will keep saying, "I don't believe You brought me this far to leave me."

Don't Become Discouraged

We talked about finding the blessing in your storm to keep you from becoming discouraged. GOD sees your pain, your confusion, and your dwindling faith. You have to think the Christian life is not all about you. It is about your faith in GOD and what you are willing to give up for Him.

When Your Load Gets Heavy

When your load gets heavy, when your feet get worn, when your soul gets weary, when your eyes get tired of shedding tears because of darts that have been fired, and the muck of life in which you find yourself mired, keep stepping, in Jesus's name.

Remember, He sees; He knows; He cares, And only "mustard seed" faith is required!

I want to talk to you briefly about three things: skipping faith, tottering faith, and "ultimately" faith. Here is an explanation of each, as I see things:

- **Skipping faith** is the kind of faith I had as a child when I skipped with joy quite a bit. That is why I choose to call my childhood faith skipping faith. This kind of faith propelled me onward through my charcoal-bucket, cotton-chopping, water-hauling, holey-shoes days. This was the faith that told me I was just as good as the next person, because the Lord loved me. This was the faith that told me I could and would be somebody one day if I just kept on believing in Jesus.

- **Tottering faith** is the kind that I gained as a result of life happening to me without the full benefit of the Lord's protection—in other words, when the hedges were taken down and I learned a smidgen of what life was about without that protection I had thought I would never lose. I remember thinking, some of the time, "What would I do if I ever lost this protective help that is such an integral part of my life?" Another name for this type of faith is crawling faith. In this stage of faith, you learn just how helpless you are without Him, but you keep moving toward Him, even when you have to crawl.

- **"Ultimately" faith** is that kind of faith that has seen hardships and knows what the loss of the protective hedges can do to a life. This is the kind of faith that says, "One day, He's going to wipe all my tears away if I just remain faithful and keep moving toward Him and Heaven, my home." This is the stage when we tearfully rejoice because the hedges have been put back in place, and a battle-scarred and weary soldier can have her wounds tended.

This is my walk of faith, y'all. This came to me in a moment of epiphany as I was saying my morning prayer. I hope it blessed your spirit in whatever way you needed it to, today. I make no apologies. This is who I am.

Note: I do know that **ultimately** is an adverb and that I am using it incorrectly in bullet three. But using it this way epitomizes what the word does for me. It says to me, though things are happening and have happened in my life that I just do not understand, GOD does. Words that end in "-ly" tell how and to what degree something is done. Adverbs are used to modify a verb, an adjective, or another adverb and are often used to show degree, manner, place, or time. When I see this word or hear it, it says to me that the Master Planner has everything under control. Because of His meticulous planning for my life, He has "jic's" (just-in-case's) in place for all contingencies; He has care packages available for me and messengers ready to deliver them to me according to all the "-ly's" in my life.

Ultimately

As a young person, when I first went to college, I knew what my life was about. I knew what I wanted to be. I had my life plans all laid out.

I knew the number of kids I would someday have. I knew the type of home I would someday buy, For I had grabbed life by the tail, And I was reaching for the sky.

What I didn't realize was that it was not all about me. It was about my life PLANNER, The GOD of all eternity.

When I wanted to go left but had to go right, I shrugged off the inconvenience and kept my well-laid plans within my sight.

When I tripped and fell while running my race, I picked myself up, dusted my knees, and wiped my face.

I kept skipping along, though I had to hobble now and again. I kept moving toward my dreams,

Though sometimes I was too winded to sing my song.

By the time I had climbed a few mountains and labored up some hills, I began to wonder to myself, "Hey! Wonder what's up; what gives? For this is not the type of life I had planned to live."

Then I thought about Jonah from the Bible days, who had not wanted to do GOD's bidding, who wanted to follow His own ways.

But that was Jonah, and I am me. Besides, the GOD of the Bible does not have special plans for me.

HE deals with superstars like David, Daniel, Elijah, and the Hebrew

Boys. He does not bother with folk like you and me, who have always been free to do whatever we enjoyed.

Then why are all these things happening to me? An elderly neighbor said to me one day, "You are not your own boss. Jesus has the final say. Plans were made for you way before you were born. You have to take your faith in your hand and begin your GOD-planned sojourn. You see, Jeremiah 29:11 says the Lord does have plans for you. So, baby girl, just you wait and see where HE leads you."

Yes ultimately, HE has the final say. I'm just glad that HE gives us time to change our planned route According to what HIS plans say.

Though this day be filled with chaos and storms, I know that this page is but one from the plan book that was written before I was born.

So, I'll not worry about what's coming ahead, because just like the lilies of the field and the sparrows of the air, HE has always kept me clothed and has always kept me fed.

I'll just lean on HIM, because ultimately, HE cares for me; I know because HE finished this story of mine a long time ago.

Ultimately, ultimately— what a word; what a word. One of the most beautiful words that I have ever heard.

So, I would not change one step of my journey, as I found the path for my life. I'll just hold on to "ultimately" and say... ♪♪♪ "Ultimately, oh-h-h ultimately Ultimately, oh-h-h ultimately GOD has a plan, a plan for me And the name of that plan, I call 'Ultimately.'"

When I wrote the poem above, it had such an impact on upon my life that I made a song out of it! I wanted the masses to praise Him and get enjoyment and encouragement from the words, too.

If it has not already been released to YouTube, it will be shortly. I thank GOD for giving us the gift of song so that we can sing our cares away and offer praise to Him at the same time.

Aside: GOD finds superstars among common folk. Just sayin'—you never know the reason behind your storm.

Let's always be mindful of the fact that when we go through things that we think are just horrible, they may actually be the avenue to our blessings. Remember Abraham (Genesis 22:9–13, 17 NKJV).
Also, Paul and Silas used songs to help them through their storm of being imprisoned (Acts 16:25–34 NKJV).

Yesterday, the singing took my joy to soulful new heights. There is something about singing that lifts our spirits faster than most anything can. I agree with the psalmist, who said in Psalm 81:1, "Sing aloud unto GOD our strength: make a joyful noise unto the GOD of Jacob; I will sing of the mercies of the Lord forever: with my mouth will I make known Thy faithfulness to all generations" (89:1 KJV) and "O come, let us sing unto the Lord: let us make a joyful noise to the Rock of our salvation" (Psalm 95:1 NKJV).

When you put your heart into your singing, a contagion of joy seeps from your soul and soars through the air, enrapturing all who are present. I hope your worship was as uplifting as the one I was a part of yesterday. We had a hallelujah good time and gave GOD some praise.

Earlier, I talked to you about the other side of "through." When it's over—when it is all over—then the celebration will begin. And you will celebrate! I know; been there, done that.

Yes, storms will come from time to time, with various intensity levels. But think about this: remember Job in the Bible? The worst part of his storms was the last part. That, my friend, lets you know that you must be close to "the other side of through" (i.e., your storm being over). Another way to say this is, "It's always darkest before the dawn."

So tell yourself, "I can and will make it, because I trust Him to lead me to the 'other side of through.'"

If you wait, come what may, you will have a brighter day, for no storm lasts always.

Just lean on His plans for you, And He will make a way.

Discussion Questions

1. Why was the book of Job written?

2. Does the adversary know who is the most committed to GOD?

3. Do you believe that you can be hit by a storm, be blessed yourself, and help someone else at the same time?

4. Are GOD's people ever in fear for their lives because of serving Him? (1 Samuel 22:1 NKJV)

5. GOD used a burning bush to gain Moses's attention, and He made the winds and water bend to His will and got the disciples' attention. Does He use measures like that today?

For Further Reading:

Psalm 27:14, Isaiah 40:31, Romans 5:3–5, Psalm 5:11–12, Romans 5:35, Job 23:10, 1 Peter 1:7–17 NKJ

Devotional:
You Can Do It

"Smoke! Somebody smells like smoke. Yuck!"

Alicia thought to herself, "One day, my clothes won't smell like smoke and one day…"

Alicia went into her favorite pastime for when she was bored. She daydreamed!

"Alicia! Alicia Nicole Brown! Name the different types of prepositional phrases and give the class an example of one in a sentence."

"Uh-oh," she thought, as she stood up beside her chair. "I only glanced over that page!"

She looked at Hank Gould, who had his usual "ready to laugh at you smirk" pasted on his face.

"I'll show him. Please make me remember what was on that page," she muttered to herself.

Alicia looked out of the corner of her eyes toward the ceiling and began to tell the types of prepositional phrases there were, as the page she had scanned slowly came into view in her mind's eye. She gave a sentence with a gerund phrase, looked at Hank Gould with a "Not today, you don't laugh at me," smile and triumphantly flopped back down into her seat.

"Nicely done, Ms. Brown, but try to keep up with the class. You might not get lucky next time."

"Yes, Ma'am," Alicia meekly murmured. She stole a look at Hank Gould and stuck her tongue out at him.

He looked at Alicia with a "mess with me look" and blurted out, "Ms. Felicity, smells like something is burning and it's hurting my nose."

Hank gave Alicia his best, "Now top that one, Girlie" glares.

The other kids chimed in, "Yeah, it does. I smelled it when I was passing out papers." "Yeah, it's been smelling like that all week."

Alicia dropped her head as her eyes slowly welled up with tears.

"That's enough class," said Ms. Felicity sternly. "It is probably a ballast in the lights going bad."

Alicia glanced at Ms. Felicity and gave her a tremulous smile of thanks.

When the bell rang for class to be over, Hank walked by Alicia and whispered, "Cry baby!" then snickering as he left the room.

'Sniff! Sniff!" Alicia trudged slowly home. She could not walk slow long though, because the wind was cutting her in two!

She put her armload of books down on the sidewalk and buttoned her coat and put her head scarf on.

Then Alicia picked up her books, wiped her eyes and running nose on her sleeve, and kept pushing against the wind on her way home.

As she walked, she thought about what had happened in the last period class. "Maybe they will have forgotten about it by tomorrow," she thought. But with Hank Gould around, she knew not to count on it.

"One day," Alicia thought, "I'm going to be somebody; see if I don't," she muttered to herself. Alicia was so cold that she wished some of the cars passing by would stop and offer her a ride. She did not mind the three mile walk on most days, but during the winter, it was rough.

She settled into her walking routine being sure not to step on the loose pebbles on the sidewalk because she had learned early on that those loose pebbles hurt quite a bit when your feet are nearly numb with cold. Alicia quickened her step. She was thinking that she would be glad to get home so that she would be out of the wind. Whew, it was cold!

She had to pass a local consumer store every day on her way home and she passed it today, she saw a mound of shoe boxes piled up next to the dumpster. Alicia crossed the street and started going through the mound of shoebox trash. Lucky day! She even found a shopping bag with two handles almost intact. She left that dumpster with a hefty shopping bag full of smashed shoeboxes, their tops and the accompanying tissue paper inserts. She wished that her brothers had been with her; then they could have brought all the boxes home. Alicia sighed and was thankful to have been able to get the ones that she had gotten.

(Rip-p-p!) The loose handle on the shopping bag ripped just as Alicia started across her front yard. She tried to juggle books, boxes, and her pocketbook. She lost the battle with all three. Alicia was only a little bit embarrassed to have dropped her boxes. "So what; they see the empty boxes," she thought. "They could be for a school project couldn't they?"

But Alicia knew that she was not fooling anyone. She knew that everybody knew that their lights were turned off, in fact, probably had been peeping out of the window when the MLGW truck pulled the electric meters and turned the water off at the curb. They always made so much noise when they turned off the water. It was almost like they enjoyed clanking that long metal thing against the water cover like it was a gong. "Boy, they must really enjoy their job," was what Alicia had thought on more than one occasion.

She was glad to get into the house out of the wind. She was also glad to rid her aching arms of her cumbersome burden. She looked at the little gas stove in the living room and wished she could will it to come on. "Your daydreams are not going to get this charcoal bucket going," she thought.

Now that she had the charcoal bucket lit, Alicia reached over to put the rice in the small sauce pan that Momma had named "the rice pot." Well, wouldn't you know it; the water canister was empty." Leave it to her brothers, drat them! Well, nothing to do but get the canisters and get down to Auntie Bessie's house before it got dark and get some water," she thought. Back out into the wind she went. The walk to her aunt's house was about a block long on one street and about a half a block long on the other street. "I'm going to be somebody one day; see if I don't," she thought. "See if I don't!"

She hoped her cousins wouldn't give her a hard time about the water. She knew that her aunt had started dropping hints about how high her water bill had been being. She made it to her aunt's and knocked on the door.

"Who is it?" her favorite cousin called from within.

"It's me," piped Alicia.

"Doors open; come on in."

Alicia went inside and started her routine of filling up the two canisters.

"Don't you ever get embarrassed about hauling that water? I wouldn't do it. That's what your brothers ought to be doing!" said her cousin.

"I know that's what my brothers ought to be doing," said Alicia. "But it's hard for Momma to make them do anything. You know they're teenagers and she can't make them do what she wants them to do and sometimes they make her cry. Somebody's gotta help Momma. So, I do it. I don't want to see her cry. Sometimes I hear her crying at night and I don't like to hear Momma cry. So you know; I go get the water. It's okay. Now, about people laughing at me, they gotta laugh at something. If they didn't laugh at me, then they would be laughing at somebody else. Anyway, one day I'm gonna be somebody!"

She hoped that she didn't meet any of her friends on the way home because you could hear the water splashing against the sides of the canisters. Alicia's coat was wet on one side by the time she got back home because one of the canisters had developed a slow leak. She hung the coat up on the back of the door in the bedroom and closed the door. She hoped it would be dry tomorrow because that was the only coat she had. It was so cold in the bedroom that maybe her coat would not be dry, but she had to take the chance and leave it in the bedroom with the door closed because she didn't want to smell like smoke when she went to school the next day.

Alicia couldn't worry about Hank Gould nor anybody else, right then. She had to cook. She knew it would do no good to worry about him.

Alicia went back in the front room and put the rice on in the rice pot, while she rinsed the chicken with a cup of water. When the rice got done, Alicia set the rice on her makeshift table, the metal chair that was beside the charcoal bucket.

Since there was no flour, she battered the chicken in meal and then put the frying pan on with a small amount of lard to cook the chicken in. Alicia remembered to use a very small amount of lard because she knew that the lard had to last for three or four weeks.

Momma had taught Alicia how to stretch the lard. She knew to use the fatback grease for cooking cornbread. And she knew to put the fatback grease back in the grease can after she finished frying anything. She browned the chicken on both sides and then poured the extra grease into the grease can. She then put one glass of water and one fourth of an onion in the frying pan to let the chicken simmer. Alicia had to be careful that the water from the frying pan did not boil over onto the charcoal and put the fire out. She knew that the room would be colder than it already was, if the charcoal got wet.

Then Alicia put more charcoal onto the charcoal bucket to warm the room a bit more.

Alicia got sick to her stomach because of the fumes from the just started charcoal. She had to go to the door to stick her head out to get fresh air so that she wouldn't be sick.

She always kept a headache in the evenings because of the fumes from the charcoal bucket.

After she had finished cooking, Alicia, again thought about her harrowing day at school. "But, that's alright. That's okay," thought Alicia. "One day, I'm going to be somebody and I'm going to have pretty clothes and ain't nobody going to laugh at me then!"

*****

Many of those high school days and nights long after her mother had fallen asleep, Alicia would go to sleep herself, with her mother's words resounding in her brain and her prayers to Jesus on her lips. "Reach for the stars; I'm going to be somebody someday! Please help me to do it Jesus, please help me." (zz-z-z-z)

And she did just what she said she was going to do. She was a good student; stayed in school; graduated from high school with a small scholarship to college and went on to become a successful teacher. (Note: The only charcoal buckets in her life now are one of the numerous grills she owns. Alicia's life story says that if you persevere with GOD on your side, all things are possible. Romans 8:28 says, "All things work together for good for those that love the Lord" and Alicia Cothran is a prime example of that…

I hope you enjoyed the story dealing with perseverance and I hope that you enjoy the poems that are in this section of the book, as I have given you a chapter from Alicia Cothran's life, during a time when she had to persevere. I further hope that this book touches an answering cord in you and resonates to you, the fact that prayer to Jesus changes things if you only persevere.

(from Chopping My Row)

****

Poem
It's a Wrap

Intro to Poem, "It's a Wrap"

Perseverance and prayer pay off. You know that? When you keep your faith and continue to persevere, it is so sweet when you get one of those tailor-made blessings that has your name written all over it! Tailor-made blessings come in all sizes, big and small. But I'm just so grateful for reminders that the Lord is mindful of me. It makes me feel so special, like I'm one in a million!

It's a Wrap ...

A tiny pebble was tossed into a dry season riverbed

As it lay there unmoving day by day

The rainy season returned with its plenteous deluge

And the headwaters of the river grew as with raindrops

Aplenty it was fed.

The headwaters became a rushing mighty torrent

And swept all on its path toward the river's mouth

To meet the ocean's mighty current.

The pebble had been worn smooth

By the mighty headwater's toss

And came forth a polished stone with a gloss

Alma L. Carr-Jones

To travel with the ocean, the whole world around

Until such time as it was deposited upon a distant shore

And by a collector, at last, was found.

It was taken home and put among the finder's rare baubles

That had been discovered of old

Well, wouldn't you know it, that shiny pebble

Turned out to be genuine gold.

So, let's remember to keep our heads up, no matter what comes up in our lives. He sees and He knows… Remember. "All things work together for good, for those that love the Lord." Rom. 8:28

Devotional:
Momma and the Rent Man

Blam! Blam! Blam! "Momma, somebody is at the door!" Louise knew it was the rent man because he came every Sunday morning to collect the rent. She was worried because the rent man knocked like he was mad. In fact, he had left mad last Sunday when Momma did not have his $10 in rent money. Louise knew that Momma did not have the rent money today either. She wondered what he was going to say, what he was going to do... "Is he going to fuss at Momma?" Louise wondered. "Jesus, please help my Momma. She was crying last night 'cause I heard her," Louise prayed. Momma opened the door.

"Something smells good in here, Lula Mae!"

"Yes sir, I fried some chicken backs for my children this morning," said Momma.

"Well, you got my money this morning?" the rent man said.

"No sir, I don't," said Momma.

"Lula Mae, I told you last week to have my money!" the rent man snapped.

"Yes sir, you did. Can you give me one more week; I can catch up on the rent, sir."

"What is going to be so different by next week that you can have my rent money?"

"Well, sir, I do day work and I got another day this week," said Momma.

"Day work pays by the day," he said. "If you got a new day this week, you ought to have my money this morning!"

"I did have it, sir, but they came to cut the lights, gas, and water off and I had to pay it to keep my children from being cold and in the dark, sir."

"You took my money and spent it. It is not my problem about your lights! I want my money, all it by Sunday or I want my house! If you don't have my money Sunday, I will be bringing the police with me to set you out! You understand me, Lula Mae?" he yelled.

Momma cleared her throat and said, "I've always paid you on time. I have only missed these two weeks and that is because I lost all my days."

"Lula Mae, your explanations don't mean a freaking thing to me! They are just like when a dog farts. You got nothing but a bad odor. And if you got rid of some of these dogs you got around here, you might be able to pay your bills on time!" he snapped.

"Now you listen here; you can't tell me what I can or cannot have in my house! These dogs belong to my children. And the dogs don't cost nothing, because unlike some folks we feed our dogs bones, Mr. Rent Man!"

"You know what, don't bother getting the rent; I want my house vacated by Sunday!"

"Now see here Mr. Rent Man, you can't…"

"Excuse me, good morning, Mr. Rent Man." Louise spoke timidly.

"Uh, good morning, Lula's little kid." He stormed down the steps and out of the yard.

Momma closed the door and said, "Whew!"

Then she turned to Louise and her two brothers and said, "I want y'all to go down to Slugall's Grocery and get me some moving boxes after church today."

A general course of, "Aw-w Momma, do we have to?" went up.

Louise piped up and said, "I got to get my homework," because she knew what store Momma put in by her good grades.

"No argument!" Momma yelled with tears swimming in your eyes. "Okay?"

"Okay Momma," said Louise and her two brothers.

"Come on sit down on your bucket so I can comb your hair for church," said Momma.

Louise thought, "I prayed to Jesus to help Momma and I know He saw her crying last night…"

Louise ran to get the lard can that she used as a stool for when Momma was combing her hair. For once, she did not argue back, nor grumble at all, not even when Momma yanked the knot too hard in the kitchen area (the back part of the head). Louise was preoccupied.

She couldn't wait to get to church because she had to talk to Jesus.

In Church…

Hey, Jesus, It's me. You did not help Momma today and I thought that we were going to have to move. The rent man, Mr. Smith, got mad at Momma and he was yelling at her, and Momma kept saying sir to him. He kept yelling and Momma started yelling too! He told Momma that we have to move and now we have to get boxes from Sluggall's after church today. Jesus, I don't want to move. I like this neighborhood and some of the neighborhoods here in Memphis are not safe. They have people that will beat you up. Some of the neighborhoods we don't even walk through because the people are so bad. I know we don't have hot water in this house, and I know that we don't have good heat. And I know that the kitchen stove smokes up everything so badly that all the curtains and the walls are black.

But Jesus, this is home and I'd like to stay here for long time. Will you help us Jesus? I know that you can because every time I cry and talk to you and sometimes when I get worried on the inside, you fix it. I want you to fix this too, Jesus, because I don't know what to do. I'm only a little girl. I wish that I could get a job, then I could help Momma. She had tears in her eyes again this morning, Jesus, and I don't like to see my Momma cry. It makes me want to cry too. Please help our Momma. Thank you, Jesus. Amen.

Louise was quiet all through service. She didn't even look around to see who was talking or passing notes. She listened to the preacher and she didn't even get sleepy.

She was thinking about Jesus and about how she could help her Momma.

When church was over Louise went to see the next-door neighbor, Mrs. Fanniebell.

She liked Mrs. Fanniebell because she gave Louise $0.50 every Saturday to go to the store for her.

"Mrs. Fanniebell," she sort of whined, "will you give me the $0.50 for going to the store for you early?"

"Well, I don't know about that Louise," said Mrs. Fanniebell.

"But, Mrs. Fanniebell, if you don't, then we gonna have to move." Tears welled. "The Rent Man said…"

"Naw, don't tell me. I heard him yelling at your Momma. I don't know what good this $.50 will do to help you, but I'm going to give it to you because you are a good girl, and I don't want to see you cry."

"Yes ma'am." She wiped her eyes. "Thank you!" A big grin replaced the tears.

When Louise got back from over to Mrs. Fanniebell's house, she was not surprised to hear Momma say, "No need to go and get boxes today; you can get them after school tomorrow."

Louis said, "Yes, Ma'am," with a smile in her voice and on her face.

"What you smiling about?" Momma said.

"Nothing, I was just thinking about church today," said Louise.

"Now Louise," Momma said sternly, "don't go getting your hopes up; we have to move and you get yourself home from school tomorrow and get the moving boxes from Sluggall's, you hear me?"

"Yes, Ma'am." Louise lost some of her happiness because of Momma's words, but not all it. She decided to keep the happy secret that she shared with Jesus to herself. She knew; she just knew that if she could talk to the Rent Man, he would not make them move. She just knew it; she didn't know how she knew it; she just knew.

The next day school seemed so long, but Louise did not care. She had something important to do when she got out. She stopped by Sluggall's on the way home from school and picked up the four moving boxes. She asked Mr. Sluggall to let her use one of his grocery carts to haul her books and the boxes in. He did.

Louise got home; put the boxes down along with her books; grabbed her pocketbook and went back out. She was so glad that they had started the street bus to coming right in front of their house. All she had to do was walk about 500 feet to the corner and wait for the bus. She was in luck and did not have to wait long. After she found herself a seat on the bus, she watched the people as they got on and off the bus and wondered what their life was like. Then she grew tired of people watching and said another quick prayer to Jesus to add to the many times she had already prayed that day.

Okay, her stop was coming up. "Here goes; hop off," she thought. Louise's leg started shaking and her throat felt like her voice was going to come out scared and squeaky. Well she was! But she was not going to let the people inside the Cotton Exchange Building know that!

She walked up the steps, wiped her sweaty hands on her dress and went inside the door. She saw a lady and asked, in her best schoolgirl voice, where Mr. Fred Smith's office was. She told the lady, "Momma sent me to pay the rent." She hoped the lady didn't say something like I'm his secretary; you can give it to me. The lady didn't and Louise was relieved because she didn't have any money to pay anybody. All she had were her prayers to Jesus, bus fare back home and a dime to buy a stage plank cake with; that's all. She went in Mr. Smith's office and the door almost shut on her because she was so little and the door was so heavy.

Mr. Smith looked up distractedly from his desk.

"What do you want little girl?"

"Excuse me, Mr. Smith. My name is Louise and I'm Lula Mae's daughter. We live on…"

"I know where you live and I know your Momma," he interrupted.

"Yes sir, well I used my $ 0.50 that I get for going to the store for Mrs. Fanniebell to come and ask you not to make us move. Momma cried when you left and I don't like to see my mama cry. It makes me want to cry too." She sniffed then took a deep breath. "I can chop cotton to help Momma pay the rent. Will you please let us stay? I have ten cents left from the bus. I will give you that and mama will only owe you $9.90."

Mr. Smith cleared his throat and gruffly handed Louise a tissue. He said, "Okay, put the dime on the table and tell Lula Mae I will see her on Sunday. You tell her that I want $9.90!"

"Yes sir! Thank you, sir!"

Louise turned and put her dime on the table and left his office. Her legs flew down the steps. She skipped all the way out to the bus stop. She did not know, but just in case Mr. Smith was looking, she put the happy little girl step in her skipping. She knew that she was a good skipper and she knew that Jesus had come through for her again.

She thanked Him on the bus all the way home. She did not forget to pray to Jesus to let Momma not be mad at her and not to whip her. She wanted to get home before Momma did so she could cook and wash the dishes to put Momma in a good mood.

But Momma was standing in the door when she got home. She didn't look mad, but she didn't look happy. Louise put on her best 'Momma guess what?' excited skip. She said, "Momma! Momma! He said we don't have to move! Momma, he was happy. And I was not scared to ride the bus down there."

Momma looked at Louise like she had two heads and purple hair. She found the chair by the door on the front porch and sat down with a woof! Louise, ever mindful of trying to keep from getting a whipping said, "Momma, Momma, are you alright? Do I need to get you some water? Huh, Momma, huh?"

"Yeah, bring Momma some water, Pooch."

Louise skipped into the house and got the water. She knew that Momma was not going to whip her. She figured she might get fussed at a little bit but she didn't care. She had talked to Jesus, and he had answered her prayer!

When Louise handed Momma her water, Momma gave her a deadpan stare and said, "Okay, tell me how you got the money to go downtown."

"Well, Momma, after I prayed to Jesus, I thought, go ask the Rent Man not to make us move. And I got my money from Mrs. Fanniebell and I used that." Seeing Momma's mouth twitch, Louise continued in her best storytelling voice like she had heard Momma use so many times. "And I wasn't even scared, but my leg was shaking a little bit." She recounted for Momma the entire episode, even down to her happy little girl step in the middle of her skipping. She and Momma laughed about that.

A few minutes later after a quiet pause, Louise spoke gently.

"Mommuh-h?"

"What?"

Louise sheepishly, 'Prayer works don't it, Momma?"

"Yeah, I declare it does," said Momma, looking at Louise once again like she just saw her for the first time.

Later that night as she went to bed, Louise thanked Jesus for not letting Momma whip her and she thanked Him most of all for making the Rent Man be nice and letting Momma keep the house. As she sleepily drifted off, Louise wondered what would have happened if she had asked GOD to make the Rent Man give her a job…(z-z-z-z)

Louise always remembered what Momma had told her about prayer and remains a faithful, prayerful Christian to this day, for she knows that Prayer changes things!

$35 A Week

$35 a week is not very much
That is what the lady lived on
And she took care of three kids, with such
Meager earnings at this –
Life in her household was anything but bliss.
But she drove her children forward
With the determination that was fierce
Reach for the stars was what she always said
As through the homework laden night
Her strident voice would often pierce.
Her relentless struggle for her children
And her stalwart belief in GOD
Gave that tired mother more than enough
Stamina to last, even when the tide was tough.
She got her children through school
And saw them become productive young adults
She got to bump her first grandbaby on her knee
And lived to see that he was the first in a long line
Of her blessed posterity.
At the close of her long life, she looked
At her daughter with a satisfied smile
And said, I am proud of your accomplishments, daughter
And I'm glad that you took a page of learning for me
But most of all, I am thankful that the GOD of Heaven
Sent you to be my child.

A tribute to Lula M. Carr, My Mother

Discussion Questions

1. Which do you think was written first, the poem, "$35 A Week" or the story, "Momma and the Rent Man"? Why? Give evidence from the poem and from the story to substantiate your assertion.

   _____
   _____
   _____

2. In line 8 what does Reach for the Stars mean?

   _____
   _____
   _____

3. Define strident from line 10.

   _____
   _____
   _____

4. Make a biblical application to the poem. A personal one.

   _____
   _____
   _____

Alma L. Carr-Jones

Devotional:
Just Dust

I hope that you and yours are feeling well.

Mindful of the fact that I am just dust, I often find myself striving to put forth an effort great enough to extol the goodness of GOD. I have been up for quite some time doing a bit of thinking and all. I have decided that I am going to begin working on my next big project. I had been wondering which direction to go next on my author/speaker's journey. Something that a person said to me in passing yesterday made me decide to give the process of starting a serious YouTube channel an all-out effort. This will indeed be a learning process for me, so I ask you to be prayerful with me on this, my latest project. Tee hee, here we go, on the creating journey again.

I have done a poem for you this morning, and I hope that you like it.

Just Dust

She knew that she was nothing but dust

She knew she was nobody that the world extolled

But what she did not know about herself

Was that she was a precious soul

Whose leaning on the Lord, as a must

Had gained her a noted and cherished

Place among the just

And that she was beloved of the Lord.

Alma L. Carr-Jones

Even when life pushed her to the point

That she turned her face to the wall

She just did like Hezekiah did one fateful day

And remembered while facing the wall to pray.

And this is what she had to say

"Lord, no matter what life puts me through

I'll turn my head to the wall, and

Father, I will talk to You."

Just a bit of dust loving, praising, and giving GOD glory as she dares to brag on Him and tell her story.

Devotional:
Sweating Tears

Today, I want you to figure out how two poems can be cohesively tied together to make a smooth flowing explanatory narrative. Do you think that this can be done? Try your hand at it.

Poem #1:

>Chopping and building go hand in hand
>Whether a metaphysical or literal row here
>Or a home in that far away land.

My! My! What a nice juicy plum of a poem for us to sink our teeth of poetic imagery into! You agree? Let's see what you do with this one.

Poetry spans time has often been said. Does the above poem support this statement? How?

Poem #2:

To Him be the glory
Tears be done
There is a race
That must be run.

In your interpretation, don't forget to tie the titles in, as well. A nice and juicy task, don't you think?

Tie-In Explanation:

Using imagery in writing means attempting to describe something so that it appeals to our five basic senses. In talking about yesterday's poem, I tried to appeal to your sense of taste by describing the poem as a nice, juicy, plum to sink our teeth into. Um, um! I can not only picture that juicy plum but can visualize biting into it. Can't you?

Chopping, building, running a race and gardening all bring sweating to mind. If you know nothing about gardening, then let me tell you a little about it.

Back in the day, before there were any individual garden tillers, life was a bit more rustic in that most small-town folks had a garden. That garden provided food for the winter months. For that garden to grow, you had to disk up the soil, break up the clods of dirt so that the soil would hold seed. Then you had to use a hoe and a rake fork (clod buster) to make the soil fine. Then you had to plant the seed. The seed had to be planted deep enough so that the birds could not get to it. You put water in the hole or hill then you covered each hole or row over. Most planting was done in the spring of the year or early summer. You had to get up early to beat the heat. Gnats, ever present, flew around your ears with their singing selves. You had to keep a sweat rag for wiping sweat and swatting gnats. Sometimes you had to give your ears a good hand flapping to get the gnats away from your ears.

I am not that much of a gardener, but I do remember some of what I just described to you from working in my next-door neighbor's garden when I was a little girl.

What I just described to you did not sound like fun did it? Well, it was not, let me tell you. It was hot, back-breaking work. Imagine going through all that to have the crops fail, due to blight, locusts, no rain, etc. All that hard work for nothing might bring some tears of frustration. All that sweating for nothing! That might make you want to throw your hat down and stomp it and say, "Drat!" if you are a man, and shed a few tears if you are a woman or do a little of both. All I just described is representative of the physical garden. You were working so hard to grow that garden so that you could feed yourself and your family as you built a home. "The Bible says that if you do not take care of your family, you are worse than an infidel." Sweating tears, I think. (1 Timothy 5:8)

Back when our country was young, trees had to be chopped down to build log cabins for homes or sod had to be cut to be stacked just so, to make shanty cabins for the family to live in. Chop the tree/cut the sod to build a place of abode.

Now you try to live a good moral life by providing for your family and living by the Good Book, right? Why? You do that because you want to go to that better land on the other shore. You know that if you live right, you will die right and get up right to go home to live with Jesus. That means that everything that you do down here on this earth is a prerequisite to making it to Heaven. In essence, you are doing like the words of that old spiritual song and building on your mansion in the sky. The song says that you are sending up timbers. Sweating and chopping and building go hand in hand, yes indeed! You have to chop some sin out of your life to build toward the future, a home down here for your family and spanning time, a home in Heaven for you when all has been said and done.

We just walked through a lifetime in that part of the explanation for our poetry. In all things, we must remember to give the Lord the glory for all things and remember to wipe our tears and keep our feet planted on the racetrack. Bear in mind that you are trying to make it home to that other shore.

Delving into something this deep helps alleviate some of the stress and strain of life by just providing a mental get-a-way and by reminding us that we are working toward a better home.

Just a thought: When we get too hot our bodies have a mechanism built in to cool us off, and it is called sweat. When life supplies a little too much heat, and we get too hot mentally and emotionally, our bodies have been designed to alleviate some of the high temperatures of the stress of life by producing tears. Well, isn't that something, sweat, and tears - both being heat reduction processes. Could you call that sweating tears?

Alma L. Carr-Jones

Devotional:
Come Boldly unto the Throne of Grace

Good morning to all you.

I learned the following Bible verse when I was just a little girl. "For GOD so loved the world that He gave His only begotten Son that whosoever believeth in Him should not perish but have everlasting life." I don't know what Bible scholars say about it, but I think that this is the love verse of the Bible. And the second verse that I would dub the love verse is Hebrew 4:16. This is what the verse says:

"Let us therefore come boldly unto the throne of grace, that we may obtain mercy, and find grace to help in time of need."

That verse speaks to my soul, and I will tell you why. But first, let me establish the fact that I believe that the Bible is the inspired word of GOD. That being said, the verse that I quoted above makes these points to me:

- Come boldly unto the throne of grace - says come with confidence; to what, to GOD's throne; throne of grace (love). We are invited to go to the throne of the Great I AM. Folks, there is no potentate in the world, no matter what kind of audience he commands, that is as great as I AM. And He has invited us with love to approach His throne with confidence? Yep, He has!

- That we may obtain mercy, - this is where we can come to get not what we deserve but get divine favor and blessings.

- And find grace to help in time of need - means that we will find kindness and goodwill when we need it.

You may not interpret this verse exactly like I did and that is alright. It says what it says, but to me, the only girl in my Momma's family and the youngest, it wraps my needy soul in a warm down filled comforter against the cold blasts of insensitivity, hatred, jealousy, etc. Along with the blanket comes loving and nurturing words that have a soothing and healing quality in them.

After my trip to His throne, I can continue with the job that He has given me and I can do it with joy! You see, folks! I keep telling you about the joys and comforts there are in prayer. Whatever you do, never forget to pray; always make time for your Father, for He always has time for you.

Devotional:
Begin Your Day with Prayer

Hello, blessed person. It is a blessed Sunday morning indeed! You woke up in your right mind with the will to BYDWP, again I say that it is a blessed Sunday morning.

Well, to the lesson for today. Yesterday, I had the opportunity to have lunch with two great ladies, Dorethea and Ernestine. We had a birthday celebration because all three of us were born in the month of July. We talked about some old times and some modern trends of today with much laughter. There is nothing like getting together with friends who accept you with all your flaws and still love you! Thanks, ladies, we will have to do this again.

Well, my husband told me this morning that we are going home. He has been preaching for 40 years, and the decision was made this morning to go back to the congregation where it all started. Yes, we have been working in the ministerial field for a few months just past forty years, and now we are set to go back home. When we left our home congregation, we had stars in our eyes and relatively few bruises. Now, we are on our way home, battle scarred, a bit weary but guess what? We still have the stars in our eyes. We have learned to look past the now to the hope of glory. We will pitch ourselves into the work of our home congregation and work like the battle-hardened and dedicated soldiers that we are.

Yes, a new beginning for us. This will be our first worship service back home, and I don't mind telling you that I am excited! Wish us well, and you be blessed in your worship service today. And never forget, we go where we go and do what we do by GOD's will. Is there a move for us in the future? I don't know, only GOD knows...

Alma L. Carr-Jones

Devotional:
Guiding Hand

Hi, there. Just fixing myself a spot of tea. Be right back to you in a few minutes, okay?...

I have had my spot of tea, and I am back. But before I had my tea, I had my time with Jesus, so I am ready now. And while I was talking to Him, I thanked Him for His saving grace and blessings. I asked for forgiveness of my sins. And then I acknowledged my dependence on Him as I made my request known. I told Him that I realized that by His will I had traveled to where I am now, traveled to where I had more than the one dress and one pair of shoes that I started my college days with; traveled to where I did not have an icebox that you had to put ice in to keep things cold but to have a refrigerator at both ends of the house; traveled to where I have central heat and a convection oven instead of a charcoal bucket for heat and for the preparation of food; traveled to where instead of having to use the "2 Walker bus" there is a four-wheeled automobile in the garage, traveled to where there was not grass growing knee high in the yard because a riding mower keeps it cut.

Yes, y'all, I talked to my Father this morning as I do every morning, yet this morning, I spent more time with Him, and I want to tell you that I came away satisfied. You see, I was burdened when I went to Him, but now I have relief. As I talked to Him, I realized that I have what I have and have come where I have come, by His will. I understood that His will has been propelling me all my life, that it didn't just start now, that I realize and recognize that He is.

I had me an inspiring, good time while praising Him for His will. I told Him that I knew that by His will, <u>mountains had been moved and storms had been stilled.</u> I made the acknowledgment to the Lord that in His will, I place my trust. That means that since, by His will, I have come thus far and I like the outcome, then by His will I am willing to be led and I trust in the ultimate outcome of it in my present situation, as well.

Alma L. Carr-Jones

I have included a poem that I penned a year ago. I pray that it blesses you and yours.

Guiding Hand

When youth allowed me to skip with alacrity
You were there watching me as I, with glee
Noticed all the things there were for me to see.

You pulled me back from things that I didn't need
And shook me with gentleness when wayward I would be
You allowed me to appease my curiosity
While lessons of insight, you did me feed.

Like the beneficent Father that You are
You guided this little one on toward the
Place that You had determined I would be
With gentle hands, oh GOD, who formed me.

There is that within me that yearns to get out
The praise that You deserve so much
For the omniscience that is You, Lord
Whose hands guide me with Your gentle touch.

Supped from the table prepared by Your hand
Great Father, GOD, Savior of man
Thank You for allowing the girl I used to be
To have grown into a lady who, with insight, can stand
To gaze into Your glory, oh GOD of my homeland
And work as I wait to be gathered back again.

Devotional:
Faith Moves Mountains

"To one who has faith, no explanation, is necessary.

To one without faith, no explanation is possible."

– Thomas Aquinas

It has often been said that "faith moves mountains." I thought about that saying this morning and this is what I came up with when I analyzed it, "If you believe in something with all your heart, you will not let anything nor anybody keep you from attempting to accomplish it, gain it, etc." What you will do is, take the venture, project, etc. apart and work on tiny aspects of it. You will work it out one step at a time but will always keep striving to reach the big picture that you carry in your heart.

One step at a time brings to mind the poem I wrote:

You

Hold on

To that dream

Don't you dare let

Anyone steal it, no matter

How dire situations seem, for

I have found that events in life are

Often like climbing up stairs that you

Though, eager must take one step at a time.

You see that I built that poem in the shape of stairs. And how do you get to the top of the stairs, exactly, one step at a time! So too, is our life as a Christian. We must learn to persevere and remember that, despite our failing attempts, we must keep trying. For, there once was a time when you could not navigate stairs, but you kept on trying. And now look at you! Going up those stairs without giving it a second thought.

Just a little something to think about. What! What did you just say? Aw, come on now... Well, you may not remember trying to learn to climb steps, but wired as I am, I remember it. I remember wanting my Momma or my daddy to pick me up and carry me up those things and I remember feeling lost when they went up them without me (though it was only three steps). I remember crying and thinking that I was going to fall, but I remember learning to crawl up them to reach my Momma's or my daddy's arms. Then came the task of learning to go down the steps! I remember learning to sit down and put my feet on the next step going down and scooting down to that step. I remember looking back at that step and doing the same thing for the next step except, I remember using my hands to leverage me up and let me down on the next step in a gentle fashion so as to not scrap my back this time. Ye-e-es, I see that it is beginning to come back to you. I thought so. We can look back on those days of learning and smile now, can't we? Sure we can, and you know what?

Here's another point to bear in mind as you navigate the twists, turns and situations of this life (i.e., climb steps to get to where we are going). Just like your parents taught you, with love, to navigate those stairs by first teaching you to go up one step at a time, and next teaching you to go down them, our Lord does the same thing. He teaches us to navigate steps in preparation for navigating stairs, in preparation for carrying loads up and down those stairs, in preparation for, one day going up those Heavenly stairs to live with Him forevermore. Ah-h-h, yes. What are a few steps when compared to that?

Devotional:
The Glory of GOD

I was talking with a friend from Florida and she told me several times during our conversation that she was so proud of me and for me. I mean, we were having an ordinary run of the mill chat and she would just burst out with, "My friend, an author! I can't believe it!" Or she would say, "Girl, I can't believe you're an author." Or she'd say, "an author and you're good, too!" Each time she'd do that it broke my train of thought, and I would have to refocus my thoughts back on the conversation. Then we focused on my writing and my willingness to help a Christian school charity of mine. She said, "See, that is why you are being blessed, because to you, it's not all about you." I chuckled and I told her as I have you and so many others, "Anything that I do well, let's be clear about this, it's not me, but the glory of GOD shining through me." To which she replied, "My point exactly."

And you know folks, she was right. Let's all remember to give Him glory in all things that we do well, and try to show that glory in our everyday lives, as well.

What areas of your life has GOD gifted you? How do you use those gifts to glorify Him?

Devotional:
Another Step on the Road to Ultimately

Good morning, all! Today is another stop on our road to ultimately. Thank You, Lord, for another "ultimate" day. If you think about it, I mean really think about it, you will realize that each day that we live is propelling us onward toward our destination of "ultimately." Either in Heaven or hell, we will lift up our eyes. We are preparing each day we live for the answer we will give when our name is called. We are preparing for eternal agony or eternal bliss.

Here are a couple of things to ponder about concerning another ultimate day:

- Plan book: pages therein are preset. Each day is a gift that we use as building blocks on our road home. A good song for this pondering point is, "Sending Up My Timbers."

- Marches on: Nothing lasts forever, not us, and not even bad old trouble. It all represents the passage of time, which waits for no man. "It is once appointed unto man to die and after that, the judgment." Song - "I'm So Glad, Trouble Don't Last Always."

- One day - The Creator, Himself, will touch the thing He created and gently wipe the tears from the eyes. I don't know about you, but folks, I just want to revel in the touch of my Master's hands as He wipes everything alright for me. That means that trouble will be wiped away; pain wiped away; sorrow wiped away; racism wiped away; hatred wiped away, etc. Song - Walk Around Heaven All Day."

In short folks, I am thankful to be given one more day for building for Him as He prepares for me, a home. When I get there, I can enjoy the things He has prepared for me that cannot enter into my mind and my heart because it surpasses my understanding. Don't you know that nothing this life has thrown at us will matter then? Ah, in the hands of my Jesus, that will be enough for me.

I thought about doing a poem for you today but then thought better about it. Nuf said already! The cakes that I baked up for you today needs no poetic icing. It is sweet enough! Ah-h-h, how sweet it is and how sweet it will be!

Devotional:
Improving Today for All My Tomorrows

Improving today for all my tomorrows
For tomorrow's man, me, does follow.

If a person is a body builder or has lifted hay bales most of his life, you don't have to hear him say a thing to you before you can ascertain the fact that you have a strong physical specimen in front of you, do you? No, you don't. The physical body speaks for itself.

By the same token, when you wrestle with problem upon problem and weather gales and storms with faith and trust that says "The Lord will take care of all my trials," you will get to where the things that bother most folks just don't bother you. Your spiritual body will start to be seen in a light similar to the physical body builder. You may be surprised one day to hear somebody say, "How do you do it? How do you stay so strong in your belief in the Lord with all that has gone on in your life?" This thought may make you reflect upon the spiritual message of faith that you are sending to your fellowman.

We've talked about this very thing on my blog in the past. We've also talked about how the Lord gets us ready for whatever plans He has for us according to His purpose. What I mean is this: He does not have to get our permission to begin or continue to carry out His plans for us. He does not have to ask our permission for anything. What we have to do, as His servants, is keep our faith in Him intact, no matter what unforeseen circumstances occur in our lives.

Keeping your faith intact in trying times is an easy thing to say, but it is not an easy thing to do. I will use myself as an example. Back when I got hit with a supercell of a storm in my life, I cried, prayed, was frustrated, wondered why all that stuff was happening to me and railed at the fates, all while trying to keep my faith in GOD intact. I kept thinking in my mind and sometimes saying to myself aloud, "All things work together for good for those that love the Lord." (Rom. 8:28) Since I knew that there was no question of my Love for the Lord, I figured that the fault had to have been in my understanding of the portion of the Scripture that said: "All things work together for good."

I even used to ask myself, "Now, what good can come out of this?" Those are the words of a person whose faith is being severely challenged. The words suggest, "Now, I'm getting tired of this. This isn't fair, and it is not supposed to be this way. I have had enough of you, trouble, so go pick on somebody else. I'm serving GOD. Go find some of those folks who are not. And if things did not let up after several long praying sessions, I thought, "GOD is not hearing me; what good is it doing me to pray? What good is it doing me to be faithful to Him? He does not care about me because He is not answering my prayers. He even lets my enemies laugh at me for being so sanctimonious."

Yep, there are times in all our lives that we forget to remember the way that the Lord has brought us over, we forget to remember how sweetly He has delivered us before. Sometimes we get so impatient that we think, "That was then: this is now. What has He done for me lately? He has taken His love and protection from around me."

Nope! Nope! Nope! As my mother told me time and time again, "You have to keep trusting in Him even when it seems that you have no reason to trust." We must remember that "The eyes of the Lord are over the righteous and His ears are open to their cry."

You cannot ask, "Then why is He letting all this happen to me if He loves me so much?" Listen to yourself. Do you hear what you are saying? Have you forgotten that He loves displays of faith? Are you telling the Creator of the universe that He has to ask your permission before He can do anything with your life? He does not have to tell you beforehand that, "I am going to put you through some faith strength training exercises. You just stay with me and though the fire will get hot and mighty uncomfortable, I won't let you burn. If you will work with Me, when I finish with you, you will shine for Me, as never before. Is that alright with you?"

Where is your faith, that "Substance of things hoped for, the evidence of things not seen?" It is no small wonder that Jesus said, "Oh ye of little faith." Yes, folks, I have had that discourse with myself on several occasions. After such a discourse, I would find myself reading that chapter in the book of Job where the Lord asked Job, "Where were you when I laid the foundations of the earth, where were you when..." (Job 38:4) After I had read that chapter, I hung my head and thought, "Thy will be done Lord; thy will be done, but please keep holding my hand because this is more than I can stand." After such times, I would call to mind the Scripture that says, "I can do all things through Christ Jesus, Who strengthens me." (Philippians 4:13)

Why am I saying these things to you? I am saying them because we live in a world where some people have very little regard for human life; a world where people do not care about basic kindness to one another, where kindness is perceived as weakness; a world where it is all about I, me and my, and no matter who has to be stepped on, as long as I get what I want, etc.

So, we have to keep our faith intact and let others see us trying to be faithful, loving, and caring, taking the low road out, etc. If we do this, we will be shouting our love for Him and mankind, though the world thinks they don't want to hear it or don't have time right now for it. We have to keep sending a positive message to the world by listening to the message of faith in GOD from our forefathers that says, "He will make everything alright." That's what my Momma always said; my Gran Gran always said, and the Bible still says!

Y'all, enjoy your day and stay prayed up.

*Endeavoring to encourage you today
and leave a positive message
for the man of tomorrow.*

Alma L. Carr-Jones

Devotional Poem:
Your Name I Do Praise

Hello, all! Had a grand time praising Him in song and worshiping Him on yesterday. I hope that you did, too. Here is a poem for you to enjoy as we lift our Lord's Name toward the sky.

Walked through valleys deep and wide

Ladened with pitfalls that managed

To make me break my stride

Rested along riverbanks and cried

'Til Your loving Presence, being felt by my side

Took my hand and became my guide.

Your name I do praise

With Your banner hoisted high

As awareness of Your phenomenal love

Among men, I do raise.

Alma L. Carr-Jones

Poem

His Will

If they say you can't

If they say you won't

Just you remember that

GOD says it best and

If it's His will

You will

Not won't.

Poem

My Father

The GOD that I am privileged to serve
Is awesome in HIS power
And you know what is so good about HIM
Is that I can call HIM any hour.

I can call HIM in the morning, at noon time
Or even late at night;
I can call HIM about my problems and
HE makes everything all right.

Now don't get me wrong, I don't serve HIM
Simply because of what HE can do for me,
I serve HIM because HE IS and HE
Holds the key to/for all humanity.

There is something within my soul
That makes me want to shout,
"My GOD is an awesome GOD
Of that, there is no doubt!"

I was trying to get this down on paper
Before it had grown cold,
But pen and paper can't do HIM justice
HIS glory is untold.

HE is my FATHER, FRIEND and CONFIDANTE;
HE is my all in all;
I wish that you knew HIM like me
And could heed HIS loving call.

Alma L. Carr-Jones

HIS love is indescribable;
It's like a gentle balm,
That no matter what I go through,
Instills a gentle calm,

You see, HE makes my enemies leave me alone
When I become so weary,
That I feel that I cannot go on because
My eyes have gotten so teary.

It's like HE says to my enemies,
"Mess not with her; she's mine!
I do not take kindly to you bothering my
Children; I think that you will find!"

HE restores my soul, keeps me replete
And gives me enough strength
To keep my grip and stay the course,
No matter what the length.

I am trying to express my love for
And my trust in my FATHER to you,
But the truth is, I can't do HIM justice,
Even though this poem is through.

(Excerpt from AVIA)

Devotional:
Uncomfortable

I am just a country bumpkin
Still holding on to the standards
With which I was raised.

My mom was a preacher's daughter
And there were certain things that
She did not condone and would
Not allow her children to do.

Found myself thrust into a situation
Last night that made me cringe
And I thought to myself, "You
Know your mother would not be
Comfortable with the mess that
You have been put in, for she
Would say, 'No, no daughter, you
Are standing too close to the fringe.'"

So, what I did was remembered to whom I belonged,
And held my head up for all to see
The Spirit that dwells inside of me.

Good morning, all. Hope you are faring well. The poem above needs no questions to help you interpret its message. Just you remember that sometimes the world can make it awkward for you to stand on your Christian values. But you know what? You have to stand on them anyway!

Alma L. Carr-Jones

Shape Poem

Your Road

Your Road has been prepared
In readiness for your journey.
Stay on the course and you will be okay.
You will find with passage of the miles
That you have been well-equipped
For your journey Home.

Alma L. Carr-Jones

Poem

7 Days

If seven days were all the time
On earth that I had left
I would work non-stop to get all my
"Meant to" things off of the "forgive me" shelf.
I would be on fire for the LORD and would tell
Everybody I met to get their life in accord
With the way that the LORD wants us to live
I would talk repentance to liars and adulterers
And tell their wives/husbands that
They needed to forgive.
I would read my Bible every spare minute
Of the day
And remind my children/spouse
That Jesus is the way.
I would let them see and hear me praying
As I tried to live the life to back-up
What I was saying…
If you had seven final days given to you
Are those some of the things that you would do
What about the homeless, the prisoners and the sick
I bet that the problem of neglected Christian duties
Is one lollipop that you would try to lick.
If we would do all these things
If we knew we only had seven days
Then what is to keep us from starting
To change our slothful ways?

Discussion Questions

What is the theme?
_____
_____
_____

What is meant by the "Forgive me shelf"?
_____
_____
_____

Poem

The Word, "Momma"

The word, "Momma" is not one
That I can use as freely as some people do
Because I lost my Momma to a heart attack
Back on August 30, 2002

I will never forget that day that
They called me to the office and said
Mrs. Jones, we can't get Mrs. Carr to the door,
Will you go and see if she is still in bed

"She probably had a doctor's appointment or is back
In the back and didn't hear you knock"
Boy, what I didn't know was,
That I was in for a shock

I knew that my Momma was fine because
The same thing had happened just the other day
I had gotten all worried because the Meals on Wheels people
Had wanted me to go and be sure that she was okay

I asked the secretary if she could get someone
To watch my class until I got back
On my way to my Momma's house,
Speed I did not lack

I told myself, "Slow down Alma, remember
This happened just the other day
Don't get yourself all worked up because, when

Alma L. Carr-Jones

You get there you'll see that she is okay"
I drove up to my Momma's house
And inserted my key in the lock
Don't know why I did so, but I
Didn't even bother to knock

"You-u-u who-o-o", I yelled as I opened
The door and started down the hall
That was our mother/daughter way of announcing
Ourselves, when upon each other we'd call

I don't know what made me start to walk slowly,
But that is how it was
When she didn't answer me, I figured
She had gone down to visit Roz

I peeped into her bedroom and
Saw her purse on the shelf
So I kept walking and peeped around the bathroom door
And saw my Momma for myself

She was sitting fully clothed on the stool and
Had fallen halfway into the dry tub/shower
I remember saying very softly, "Oh Momma,"
And then methodical shock took over, that very hour

I remembered calling 911, telling them what I thought and
Asking if I could take one of my fingers and gently touch her back
I asked the operator if she would stay on the phone
While I ascertained the fact

I touched her back and it was hard
And I told the operator that
I don't remember what else she said but I do remember
Calling the school and making known the fact

Renewal of Joy

That I would not be back to school for a while
Because my mother was gone
The secretary asked me if I was alright
And if I were all alone

I remember screaming at her and telling her that I
Was not all right and never would be the same
I remember slamming down the phone and
Screaming over and over again.

Yes, I made it through my Momma's death
And doing what had to be done
But you know, she had told me the week before that should
Something happen to her that I would be the one

To find her body, because my brothers lived
Out of town, so I would have to be strong
I told her that I could not do that and
About me doing that, she was wrong

She calmly replied, "You're stronger than you
Think you are and you will see so too."
Yes Momma you were right, I did find you and
It was rough but I did make it through

It's been 8 years and I have finally begun my
Writing career, of which you said I would
I only just penned this poem about your death,
Because it is only now, that I could.

LORD willing, I will see you on the other side
When this life for me is through
Then I will get to shout, "Momma, Momma, Momma!"
And put my arms around you.

– In Loving Memory of Lula M. Carr

Alma L. Carr-Jones

Poem

Renewed Faith in My Fellowman

April 16, 1987 is not a date
That I'll soon forget
For the happenings of this day
Left me quite upset

I was running late so I didn't
Take time to put on my rings
I left them on my dresser with
My other jewelry things

Our house was about 7 miles from the
School where I taught Special Education
And as I drove, I enjoyed the breezy sun filled day
With a sense of quiet elation

I enjoyed the new spring green of the grass
That would soon need mowing
I enjoyed the tenacious little daffodils
That had just started growing

I chatted with my son about
What time I would pick him up
I reminded my daughter to finish her
Apple juice from her new sippy cup

After I dropped my kids off at
Their respective schools

Alma L. Carr-Jones

I hastened to my job because being
    Late was against the rules

I made it to school, went to the office,
    Said, "Hello" and signed in
Didn't have a clue that within two hours,
    I'd be back in that office again

I spoke to my colleagues as I walked
    Past each of their doors
Then I went out to the portable building
    To begin my daily chores

Of teaching reading, math, spelling
    Language, science, and social studies
And was glad to see my two new teacher's aides who
    Had turned out to be my hard-working buddies

We had all settled in for the morning and had
    Our children working as hard as could be
When the secretary interrupted our second class
    By intercom and said that she needed to see me

I said I would come as soon as the next bell rang
    And I had let my children go to P.E.
She told me to come right then and to let one of the aides
    Keep my kids and to bring the other one with me

"Wonder what's up?" I said aloud as my two aides
    And I looked at each other with puzzled eyes
"It's probably that shipment of workbooks I ordered and
    She wants them out of the office as fast as instant pie."

Well, we sped down to the office because interrupting
    Class for a workbook shipment is simply not done
When we rounded the corner of the office door, the secretary said,

"Just got a call and your house is on fire hon."
My aide started to have hysterics and
I began to try to calm her
When the secretary said, "Not your house, but (pointing at me)
Yours, while touching me on my shoulder

I stammered, "M-my house is burning down?
Nah, somebody has made a mistake"
My boss told me to go home and my aide
And another one, along with me to take

A leveled headed aide drove and when we were 5 miles
from my house,
We could see a thick black column of billowing smoke
We all watched that column but I
Was the only one who spoke

"If that's my house burning, there won't be
Anything left when we get to it, you know"
The level-headed aide said, "It's not your house because that
Fire is too close and we still have five miles to go

"Maybe you're right, some farmer is probably burning
Off his field and it got out of control"
Said the other aide, while I onto that
Slim hope tried to keep hold

You know, in the rural areas, you travel
Through so many twists and turns
But no matter how many twists and turns we made, we kept coming
Back toward that column of smoke where we could see stuff burn

Was it only my house that we
Found blazing that April day?
Nope! When we got there, my Mom's had already burned
Completely and mine was well on its way

Alma L. Carr-Jones

I stood there and watched my son's room, my
Daughter's room and our bedroom go up in flames
When I think about it, I still think
It was an awful shame

That there was no way to get a pumper there
Fast enough to pump water from the ditch
But you know how things work; they
Seldom go off without a hitch

By the time the pumper came, four
Miles from the nearest town
My little house with all its contents
Had burned to the ground

I thought about my kids pictures that
I had had taken through the years
I thought about my new teaching wardrobe and the new
Riding lawn mower and I couldn't see for the tears

I remember wondering why the
Grass didn't stop growing
I remember wondering why the wind
Just kept right on blowing

So much for my ideas about treating people right and
Doing the right thing, all that had just come up empty
Then I thought about how though the fire had taken
Her house and ours, GOD left my Mom with me

Then I remembered that we had changed insurance companies
and the old coverage
Ran out and the beginning new coverage on the
following week would fall
What week did my house burn, the week when there
Was not a single smidgeon of coverage at all

Renewal of Joy

That meant that everything that I had worked and scraped for for
Thirteen years was lost and no way to replace any of it
People kept saying, "These things can be replaced." And I thought,
"The next person that says that to me is gonna see me have a fit

Sure enough, the level-headed aide said "it" and I screamed
At her, "You just tell me how!"
"You're going home to your house intact; What cha' got to say about
that now?!"

She never said a word, but bowed her head and
Then asked me if I had called my spouse
I told her that somebody had gone home and
Phoned his job from their house

When my husband got there, he just sat on the side
Of the hill and just sobbed and sobbed
He said that he couldn't feel any worse
If we had just been robbed

The only thing that I kept saying aloud was that
I didn't even own a broom straw
And I kept wondering, in my mind, when that awful
Knot in my throat was going to start to thaw

And that level-headed aide to which
I threw a screaming fit
She only supplied my son with an entire wardrobe (shoes and all)
And even threw in a broom and dust pan kit

Furthermore, my kids' respective schools replaced Their new bikes that
we had just bought
And we were supplied with house wares, small appliances, clothes
And money from the school where I taught

Alma L. Carr-Jones

From the churches that we were affiliated with, we
Received furniture, linen, money and more
From the whole community to our family,
There was a tremendous outpour

So, we made it through it all, as victims
Of catastrophes, with time and effort, do
But the fire that happened on April 16, 1987,
Did my faith in my fellowman renew

And regarding total replacement fire insurance,
Allow me to tell you one thing more
Learned a lesson? You betcha! Now-a-days,
This family is fire insurance poor!

Devotional:
Influence

Hello, all. I hope that you BYDWP; if you didn't, there's still time. Just come on back to the devotional when you finish. I should be well into the rest of it by then. Okay?

The little third grader, Louise, jumped on what Momma said just like she did most things. Her mother took the time to explain to her that she should never ask Jesus for trivial things like a doll. She explained how special a privilege being allowed to pray to Him was.

Needless to say, I was that little third grader, and I took a lesson from that conversation that changed my life for the better. The lasting thing that I took away from that conversation with my Momma was that "If you pray to Jesus, He will hear your prayer and answer it in His own good time." I was taught to pray and learned to wait in patience for the Lord to answer my prayer(s).

That premise has carried me over many a mountain and through many stormy patches in my life as I wrote **Chopping My Row**. Learning to wait made my faith in Jesus stronger.

Somebody once said that "If you do what you have always done, you will get what you have always gotten." That is so true, but in this case, I want to use it in a positive sense. Since I have always prayed and have gotten answers aplenty, I continue to pray (i.e., I have always prayed and been helped with my problems, so I continue to pray in hopes of getting help with my current problems too.) Somebody else has said, "If it ain't broken, don't fix it.")

Just like Alicia, I had been praying and waiting for something all my life, but I didn't know when I had been given it. Some of you are probably sitting there thinking, "How can you ask for something and not know when you have received it? That is just plain illogical!" To that thought I say, hold on there, my friend. Not so fast. That very thing can happen.

Let me explain it to you a little better than I have. I had been praying since I was a child for this thing. You know what I had been praying for all that time? I had been praying for Jesus to let me be somebody one day.

That is simple enough; I know. But, at what point do you know that you are somebody? You see the audience that made me feel insecure in the first place is no longer the audience I am playing to now, is it? Nope, it's not. When I became a teacher, I was around other teachers, and I was no better or no worse that the others. I was nothing special. I was just a teacher who cared. Now, don't get me wrong; I thanked the Lord for allowing me to become a teacher, but I still was not at the top of my game yet. I didn't think, anyway. When I received Who's Who Among America's Teachers, I still didn't get it. I was just one of many. I was too busy making sure that I did all that I could to help my kids and be caring at the same time. When I did think about the prayer prayed in earnest all those years ago, it was to think, not yet. I have not arrived yet, nope not yet. I am still one among many.

When my husband became a preacher and the sisters in the church wanted to dress as I did, I thought, "No biggie." That is just because he is in the limelight. It has nothing to do with me. When I was expected to speak at Ladies' Days, that was no biggie. Many preachers' wives do that. I was one among many.

When I wrote my books, it was not until my third one that someone said something that bothered me a little. Let me tell you in a brief moment what happened. There was this young lady that I had taught and she had not seen me in a while. She threw her arms around me and squealed and said that she was so glad to see me. Then she told me that she wanted to get all three of my books. I told her that they were on Amazon, and she could get them there. She became a little hostile and said that she wanted to get her books right then because she wanted me to sign them. I told her that I didn't have any books with me. She became hostile and yelled out, "Why not?" I tried to shoosh her and told her that I did not have the money to order any more right then as I had just finished a book signing. I still didn't get the picture. I just thought that some people were so bent on telling me not to change when they were acting funny over a book. I made sure that that would not happen again. I keep books with me at all times now. Well, I don't have any right now because they cleaned me out at the ALA Conference & Exhibition in Orlando.

Now here is the finale.

Remember this that resulted in this?

As a preacher's wife, you are supposed to be able to cook. Okay, no biggie, right? Here is what happened to me not very long ago. I periodically take meals to help out various church functions. I was checking to see what was needed so that I could help another church out with their food preparation. I was told what to bring, and I said, "Okay," then I was told, "Bring some of that cornbread of yours, but leave it in the car." It was to be taken to a particular house. Another time I was told to fix some dishes but to be sure and do some cornbread because there was no cornbread for the house.

Those words about the cornbread astounded me to the point that I said aloud, but to myself, "Cornbread! It's just cornbread!" Those words took me back to 8 years old when I had to fix my first pan of cornbread. (You can find the cornbread episode in ***Chopping My Row***, pp. 66-67.)

Then it hit me. The Lord had looked down the road in my life and knew this was going to happen, so He made sure that I could cook a fine pan of bread. Then I thought about the other things that had happened in my life. I thought about the week before when a former student of mine called me a Phenomenal Woman; about the great number of responses I got when I posted something on Facebook; the number of birthday well-wishes; people's reaction to me when they hear that I am an author, etc. That is when it hit me folks, Alma Jones, the Lord has answered your prayers and allowed you to become somebody!

Wow! I was bowled over when I realized what the Lord had done in my life. Now, y'all know how introspective I can be. So, I went back through my life, and I thought about the things that I could do well now. I used to play being a teacher. I used to write stories for my friends. Even back then, folks, He was preparing me for what lay ahead. And as far as being a preacher's wife, He made sure that I was close to Him. Wow! What a wonderful, mighty GOD we serve!

Alma L. Carr-Jones

What do I do with this newfound knowledge? I make sure that I do my best to give Him glory through my daily living. Humbly, I say, "Thank You, Lord!"

To be somebody is to have influence

To have influence is to bear a burden

Whether under a microscope

Or in a fish bowl

You have to be conscious of your role.

Remember, "To whom much is given

Much is required"

You got what you wanted

What you so desired

You have reached the dream

To which you aspired.

Now, it is up to you to lead

The charge that has been given to you

What will become of the ones who

Look up to and have decide to follow you?

Your influence really is only as good as the life that you live.

About the Author

Alma L. Carr-Jones, a beloved educator, poet/author, a retired educator and a motivational speaker, lives in McKenzie, TN. She is a successful author of nine books to date. Alma loves to write because, as she is fond of saying, "It is something I was meant to do."

She is:

- An Avid Inspirational Daily Blog Writer at: www.almacarr-jonescorner.blogspot.com/
- A Highly Acclaimed Retired Teacher of 30 Years
- Author of Nine Books
- A Preacher's Wife of 40 years
- A w.o.w. (woman of work for the MASTER's use)

This Christian lady is one who really tries to live up to her motto of "Doing What I Can, While I Can." Since she is quite busy doing whatever her hands find to do, that old saying of *wearing out instead of rusting out* will be true of her. She says she wants to have made a difference in the lives of her fellowmen and to have built a legacy that will still speak, even after she is planted in the ground.

To have the treasure of this woman's work in your home is to have a loving dose of life as viewed from the eyes of a preacher's daughter's daughter and the wife of a preacher. This woman has a heart of gold with arms big enough and ears tender enough to help any soul stay encouraged as they make their way toward Heaven. Alma is such a jewel of a woman that she says, when you see her doing something that you admire, "Don't get it twisted; it is not me, but the glory of GOD shining through me."

Other Books by the Author

The Tallest Mountain Series

Get Yourself Up

Lift Up Your Voice

Bear the Good News

Available on Amazon and from the Author

Thank you
for reading our books!

Look for other books
published by

www.TMPbooks.com

*If you enjoyed this book
please remember to leave a review!*

www.ingramcontent.com/pod-product-compliance
Lightning Source LLC
Chambersburg PA
CBHW060206050426
42446CB00013B/3007